The Creatures of the World

Maddie Abbott

BookLeaf Publishing

India | USA | UK

Presentation by *BookLeaf Publishing*

Web: www.bookleafpub.com

E-mail: info@bookleafpub.com

ISBN: 9789360940676

First edition 2024

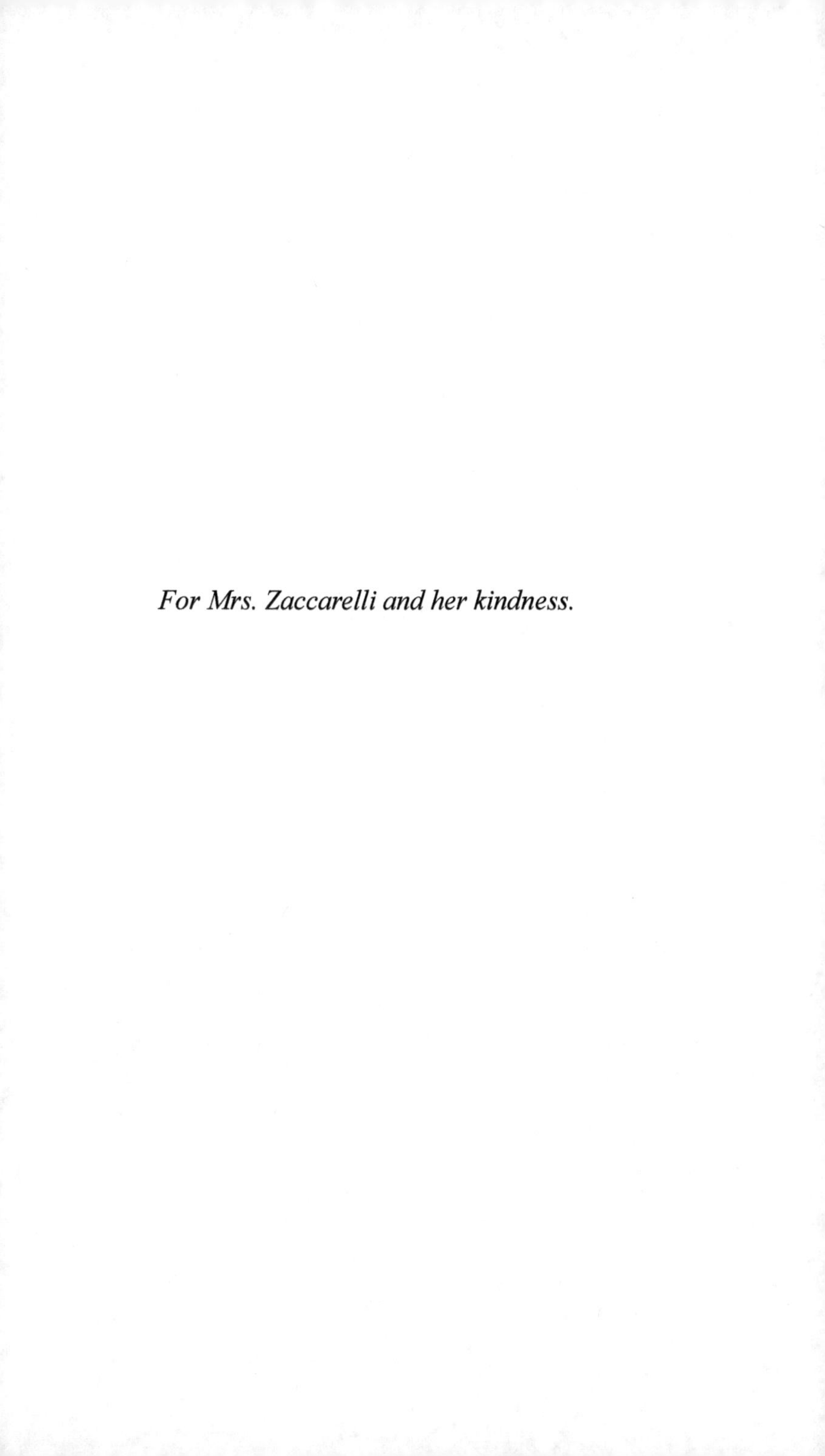

For Mrs. Zaccarelli and her kindness.

ACKNOWLEDGEMENT

First of all, I would like to thank my family, especially Mandy who helped me edit the poems to perfection, for supporting me through all of this and encouraging me when I didn't think I could come through. Thank you to all my friends that supported me and encouraged me to get this book done (and to remember to write the poems each day)! I'm also going to thank my English teachers and librarian for giving me their insight on poetry and supporting me through the making of my book. And, of course, I would like to thank BookLeaf Publishing for having this competition and publishing my book (it feels so weird to say I actually have a book!!).

The Doe

She is calm, she is peace,
She is grace, she won't cease.
She stares at the lush wood,
Not running, though she knows she should.
She beats her hooves against the snow,
Showing no fear, seeking no show.

The doe is still, not any fear on her feature,
As she stares at the new, strange creature.
In all her glory, in all her wisdom, she stays,
Experienced this only once, in all her days.
Slowly, the creature drops its spear,
As if struck by the absence of fear, in this
curious deer.

She leaps off gracefully, back to her senses,
While hopping over fresh snow on the fences.
The doe leaves the creature alone,
To pick up its spear all on its own.
As it thinks about that fearless deer,
And wonders why it was so near.

Jellyfish

No blood,
Flowing through my body.
Cutting through the deep dark,
My tentacles and I,
Just floating and floating,
Without getting anywhere.

No brain,
For me to think,
As I float meaninglessly,
Dreamlessly, through the deep dark.
Creatures among me, swimming and floating,
With brains and blood, while I have none.

No heart,
To pump life into me.
Probably why I feel so hollow,
Because I am.
No heart beating through me,
As I float aimlessly through the deep dark.

No blood, no brain, not even a heart,
I'm hollow nothingness, no purpose in life,
Except to float.
Floating aimlessly, dreamlessly, meaninglessly,

Just floating
Floating
Floating
Through the deep dark.

Stingray

Gliding through the water,
Like flying through the air.
Wishing I had some space,
In that wonderful place,
To fly through the air.

Noise, so much noise, too much noise,
Traveling through the waters around me.
I want to escape the noise and fly,
Through the sky and clouds.
The water I resent,
I want freedom in the air.

To fly, to die,
What difference does it make?
Both give me the freedom I want,
To be free from the noise of the sea.

Bald Eagle

Soaring, wind through my feathers,
Surveying the ground below.
Watching for the creatures lurking,
The creatures scheming.
Violent creatures, though they may be,
They have heart, soul, mind, like me.

Flying through the air above,
Protecting my family of three,
As I watch the creatures,
The creatures of red, white, and blue,
I see them fight to protect too.

I feel some sort of connection between,
These creatures and I.
Fighting, protecting,
watching, scheming.
These creatures of red, white, and blue,
Violent yet beautiful creatures,
Powerful and strong.
These creatures and I,
These creatures of red, white, and blue.

- This one is for the American veterans, for my Papa. Thank you for all you have done for our country.

The Rabbit

Hopping,
Through the colorful meadows.
Jumping,
In the fragrant flowers.
Feeling,
The wind through my fur as Spring comes.

Isn't it wonderful to run?
To jump?
To hop through the colors of nature?
To breathe in the essence of life?
To escape the troubles of the world?
I wish to stay this carefree forever.

Wonderful colors and smells all around me,
Wind breezing by as Spring arrives.
I stay blissfully unaware of the world,
As I bask in the essence of nature.
To jump, to hop, to skip,
All are wonderful ways to explore the world.

Whale Shark

Water, cool, confining me,
Heat from the bright Sun above me.
All is calm, all is peace,
Life is drifting past in a simple breeze,
Everything is at ease in the waters with me.

Swimming forever, never stopping,
Harming none, no enemies to hurt.
Am I a gentle giant?
Rare creatures call me that.
Knowing what they say, perhaps it is so.

The Beaver

Work, night and day,
With sticks and clay,
To make a barricade,
That the creatures haven't yet made.

This place shall be my home,
My pond, my humble abode.
While I work and work,
so my build won't erode.

My family helps me mold the sticks and clay,
So we shall someday,
Make this place our home.
Our humble abode.

I work all night,
I work all day,
Until finally, I'm done.
I made my home
Of sticks and clay.

I finished it today,
For my family and me to stay.

The Octopus

Nine brains,
Yet I feel like I have none.
Why do I feel I know nothing,
While others classify me as smart?
Nine brains and yet,
My head feels empty of all thought.
Why?

Three hearts,
Yet I feel as empty as a shell.
Why do I feel nothing?
Not an ounce of sympathy or sadness.
Three hearts and yet,
My body feels like a dried up well.
Why?

Eight arms,
Yet I feel as if I can do nothing.
Why do I feel so useless,
When others say I'm the opposite?
Eight arms and yet,
I feel everything I do is futile.
Why?

Why, oh why, am I like this?

Why does everyone have such high expectations
of me?
Why can't I meet them?
Why?
Why.
Why…

The Bat

When the sun goes down,
I come out to play.
My fur, black and brown,
Ruffles in the wind as I fly,
Through the dark sky.

I hunt in the night for food and prey,
Hearing what my brethren have to say.
Using sound and smell,
Sight disregarded,
To find my prey who fell in the night.

Sounds all around,
Soothing sounds of the night.
Wishing I could stay here in flight,
But the sun will come up soon,
And I can only fly with the moon.

The cool night air,
Ruffles my hair,
As I escape the light.
My world flips as I slip,
Into a darkness deeper than the night.

The Bee

Flying around, collecting pollen,
From the gorgeous flowers that have fallen.
My hive and I make the honey,
This delicious dish being our money.

I live to work, to serve my Queen,
Though she stays unseen.
Buzzing, buzzing noise we hear,
Everyday no other sound near.

We don't complain, we get it done,
Underneath the blazing sun.
We fly and work to support our hive,
Working and working our whole lives.

I don't mind this brutal pace,
I've grown to love this buzzy place.
The routine of yellow and black,
To my hive, I'd never turn my back.

The Lion

Hear a roar, loud and proud,
The King of the Jungle makes this sound.
It echoes throughout the bones,
Of the other animals on these stones.
The roar instills pride and fear,
In all that are near to hear.

A mane, full and long,
Showing the others how strong,
The King of the Jungle remains.
He looks out over all the plains,
Knowing he rules it all,
Knowing that he will never fall.

In his stance, he reigns his power,
Through his intimidating glower.
The King of the Jungle shows his teeth,
Reminding the danger that lies underneath.
He flashes his claws as he walks,
Daring anyone to wrong him with their talks.

The Snake

They call me wise,
They call me cunning,
Though when they see me,
they all go running.
I slither and crawl,
No limbs here at all,
Just trying to get along.

Some call me death,
Some call me healing,
Yet none really know how I'm feeling.
I slide along the ground,
Along the sand, along the grass,
Along the dirt,
Feeling indifferent, yet I'm still hurt.

They say I'm good,
They say I'm evil,
I admit sometimes I can be lethal.
I live my life,
Staying still, on my own,
Representing good and bad,
Yet I don't know what I stand for, all alone.

Do I stand for good?

Do I stand for bad?
Or am I just a creature,
Surviving it all?
I'll just stay here and slither,
Until my skin withers,
Continuing to wander alone.

Manatee

Staying here,
Nothing to fear,
I have no enemies,
I swim above the anemones.

I swim here, a big grey lump,
Covered in algae from my head to my rump.
Grazing day to day,
On the sea grass that is in the way.

I like to watch, I like to touch,
The creatures that lurk among us.
Be them big or small,
Size doesn't matter much.

Slow to move, I mostly eat,
I very much like to sleep.
Call me lazy all you want,
Though I will not weep.

Here I will stay, gentle as ever,
As if I am light as a feather.
I swim and eat and sleep,
Friends with all who crawl and creep.

The Frog

I like to jump, I like to hop,
And fall into the water with a plop.
Jumping from lily pad to lily pad,
I can never stay sad.

Catching flies all day,
I meet more frogs, yet they never stay.
Sometimes I'm lonely,
Though I try not to, pronely.

Some frogs are poison,
Though I am not.
Some like the cold,
And some like hot.

I croak for friends,
For someone, anyone,
Just to make sure my loneliness ends.
I croak and ribbit, yet I go unheard.

So I just jump and hop,
From flower to flower, leaf to leaf,
Catching fleas and flies,
Hoping for someone to come by.

The Wolf

Howls echo in the night,
As the pack tracks in the moonlight.
Paw prints form in the snowy ground,
As the pack runs and their feet pound.
Their prey calls out, crying for help,
As the pack attacks, making it yelp.

The stars guide their way,
As they trail across the field, never astray.
The snow packed earth between their paws,
Turns and scatters because of their claws.
They run as one, they run together,
No matter the time or the weather.

They survive, they thrive,
They fight to stay alive.
The pack attacks, they howl as one,
They run and hunt, not stopping for the sun.
Their fur coats shine, their eyes glow,
Forever at last, they go.

The Swan

White as light,
Or black as night,
Soft as silk,
The color of milk,
Are the beautiful swans.

Pretty as a flower,
Full of power,
Such elegant creatures,
With delicate beauty,
Are the graceful swans.

Blessed with beauty,
The product of true love,
The lightest of light,
The creature of the bright,
Are the angelic swans.

Or be cursed with darkness,
Love turned heartless,
Corrupt with power and sin,
Will do anything to win,
Are the ruined swans.

Pufferfish

I'm small,
Not very tall at all.
I'm often over-looked,
Only seen when they need to see me.
I hide away, not to be hooked,
I'm the coward of the sea.

Fear consumes my whole being,
I clumsily swim as I'm fleeing.
I'm scared,
Of all the creatures that swim,
Of all the creatures that never cared,
Of all the creatures who are grim.

I am a craven,
Not a raven,
For they are smart and brave,
And I have nothing but my cowardice.
They have the courage I crave,
While I stay here scared and nervous.

My only defense is to get bigger,
But I like to be small, have no vigor.
I try to be courageous,
But then I shrink back into myself,

As if everyone else is contagious,
Though I'm not at risk for my health.

I am the coward of the sea,
There is nothing else I'll ever be.

Hummingbird

A whirr of color goes past,
A slight hum of its wings going fast.
You see the small vibrancy,
Speeding like it has somewhere to be,
A little light full of radiancy,
Optimism all throughout thee.

Going speeding fast,
Having a blast.
Rushing through life,
Yet still enjoying it.
Happy without strife,
Flying and feeling like I fit.

Drinking nectar from fragrant flowers,
Feeling like I'm full of powers.
Humming loud and proud,
Showing off my gorgeous hue,
Wondering if I could fly on a cloud,
And throughout the beautiful blue.

The Squirrel

Scrambling up the tree,
Careful as can be,
He takes cover from everyone,
Not wanting to see anyone.

His brown fur coat shines,
Making high pitched whines,
As he climbs high,
Escaping to the sky.

Storing food in his tree,
He tries to flee,
He hates the world,
All scrunched up and curled.

He jumps from here to there,
He sees everything, everywhere.
He hides in the crook,
Of the tree, staring at the brook.

As he drifts to sleep,
He sees colors, just a peep.
He dreams of flying away,
Wishing to be a stray.

But then he wakes up,
The dreaming done.
He climbs back down,
Waiting to face reality.

The Eel

Gliding through the water,
Flowing like a liquid,
The tricksters of the sea,
Zapping at anyone,
That dares come near.

Electrifying, terrorizing,
Tricksters of the sea.
They lie, they cheat,
Though they've never been beat.
They electrify the sea.

Never trust an eel or you'll see,
The sticky lies they weave,
The tricks they pull,
And how they deceive.
Never trust the tricksters of the sea.

The Butterfly

Small and delicate,
Magical and beautiful,
Colorful and wonderful,
They flutter and fly,
Sent from the sky.

When you see one fly by,
It's a relative saying hi,
From above and beyond.
So please be kind,
To the delicate creatures from the sky.

They are a gift from the Angels,
Telling you all is okay,
With our departed friends,
And the ones we love,
Whom we dearly miss.

Flying amongst the flowers,
Or fluttering in the breeze,
You can find them,
God's gift,
For you and me.